Did You See My Eyes Mum

poems

Jazzy Green

new words {press}

A TRANS* & GENDER-EXPANSIVE POETRY PRESS

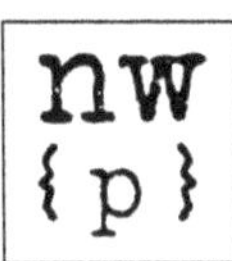

new words {press}
6030 Putnam Ave., New York, NY 11385
www.newwordspress.com | @newwordspress

new words {press} is a sponsored project of Fractured Atlas, a non-profit arts service organization with a mission of elevating emerging and established trans* and gender-expansive poetic voices, to build community, and share knowledge.

ISBN: 979-8-9903488-6-8

Cover design by Jazzy Green
Typesetting by new words {press}

Printed in the United States of America

I'd like to give thanks to all my queer friends; to all my loves, for every way they've opened the world up. With special mention to Nina, for bringing endless love and inspiration.

~ Jazzy

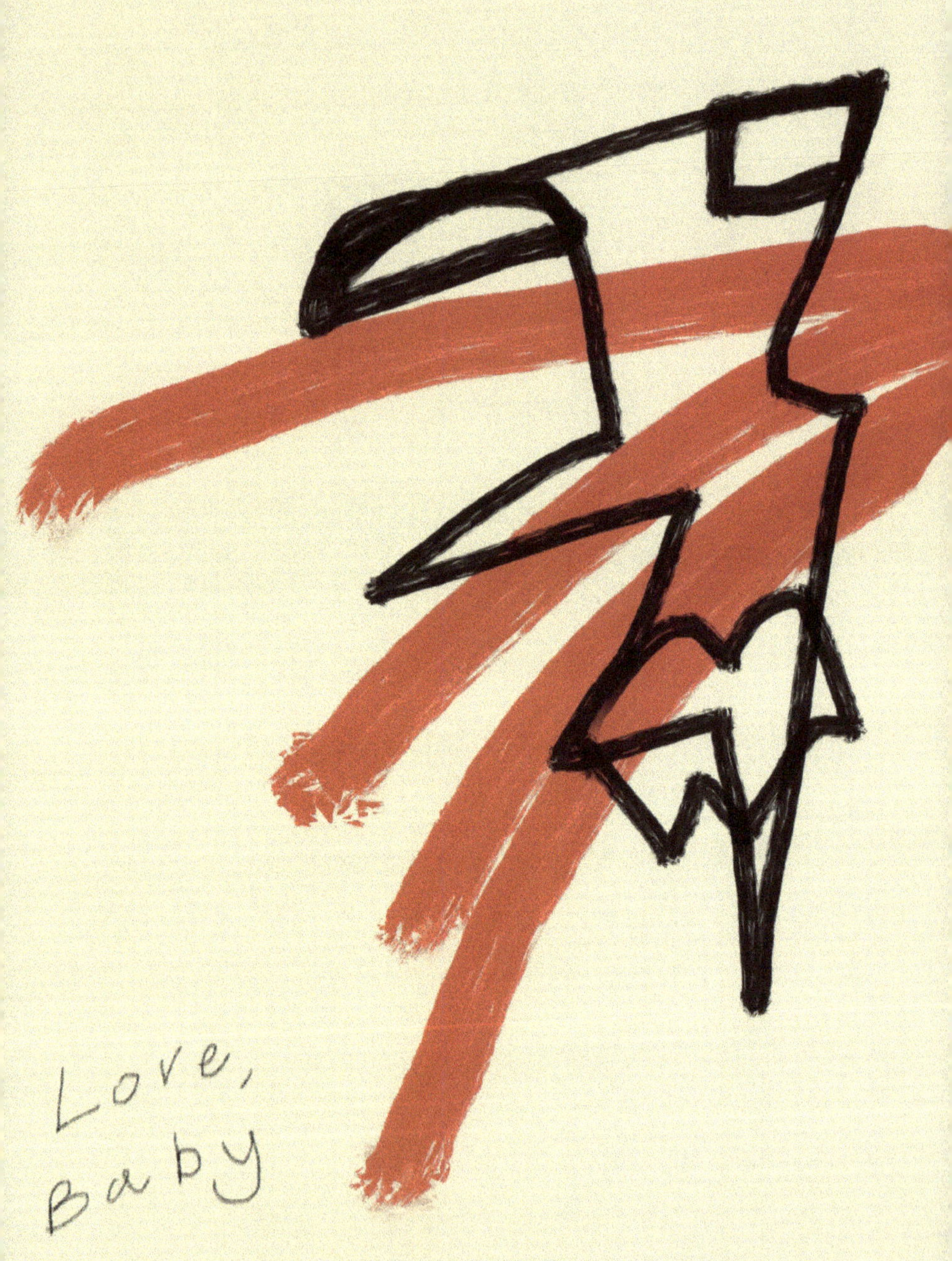
Love,
Baby

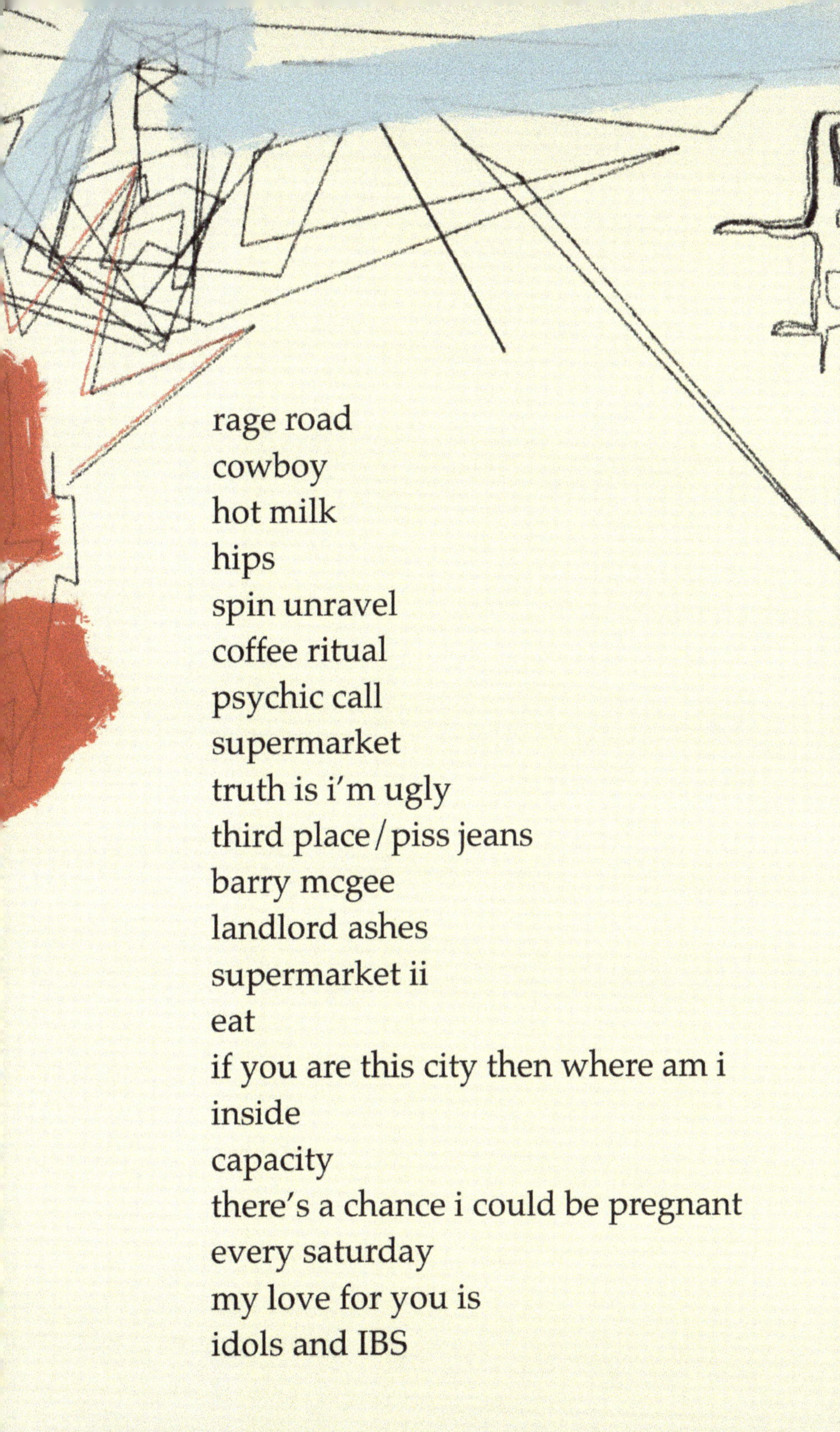

rage road
cowboy
hot milk
hips
spin unravel
coffee ritual
psychic call
supermarket
truth is i'm ugly
third place / piss jeans
barry mcgee
landlord ashes
supermarket ii
eat
if you are this city then where am i
inside
capacity
there's a chance i could be pregnant
every saturday
my love for you is
idols and IBS

Rage Road

country lanes will always be
a golf ball &
your mouth agape
dirt in the crates
a tiny violent moon
snatched from the car
door
your fist
wide as the window
winding
down the
glass ready
to spit
through hedgerows
the other guy
inside out
my narrow 9 year old mind
"Dad,
what you doing?"

tongue tied I am
your readiness
unsoothable
my bones scraping
rigid air waiting
there's no space
between you and him
now
dirty car/ your home
soft fleshy belly turning
below
my t shirt
wish I was his kid
in the back
his clean car/ a car
a family
dad why is your
car
full of
stuff?
I overspill
get your love
by swallowing this tightness

"Fairness"
you assured me
afterward -
like the air hadn't split
spitting slurs
wicker burning
quick
my trainers swing
cause they can't touch
the floor
yet
drive away fat
narrow lane
soil round fingertips
turning the dial
some Motown on
gust blown so
love returns

your smile
dirty violent swoon
    - you almost swung

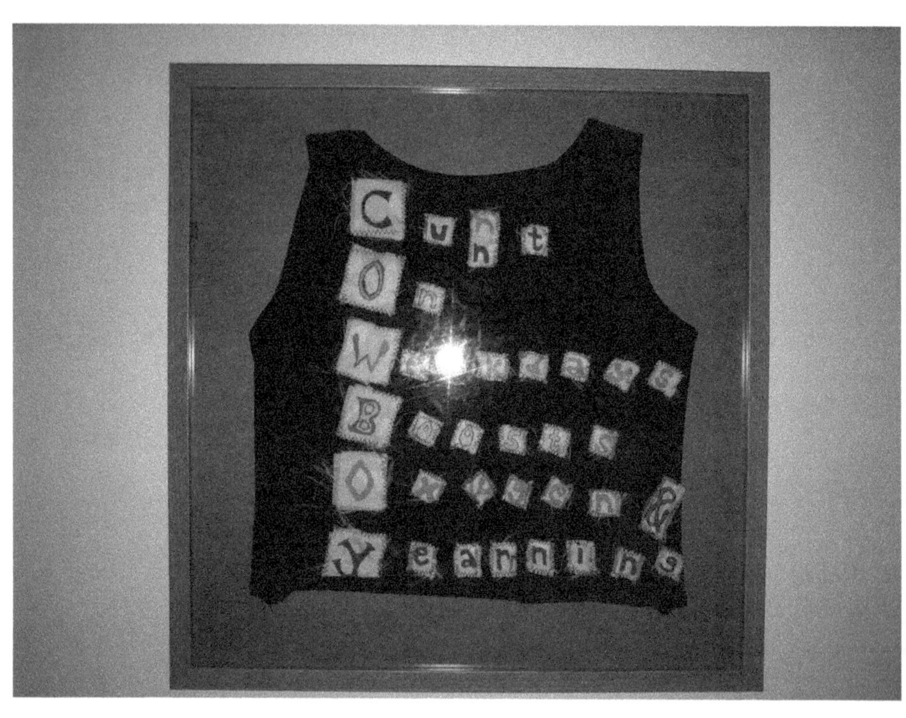

COWBOY
Cunt
Yearning

C unt
O n
W ednesdays
B oosts
O xygen &
Y earning

coffee machine whirs in circles 'round the place
2 hours ago broken
its resistance to live
snapping the routine
of many mornings
You relay the pace through pulled apart lips
inviting me to the humour of it
as milk spills across the counter
tracing back to your bedroom
floor
You'd fucked me two hours before
pressing into the wood
Your thumb beneath the fibre cloth
grains get soft and
intoxicated
Polishing happens twice daily
but not today
morning diverted with a curling tongue
Swishing 'round your mouth
the bleariness
of waking up
again

Pushing open the cafe door
out december's mouth
You remember the warmth of
mine
Slimy and making your cold fingers sting
Poking through
sudden change
like plankton
face bare n crackin' in wind
The ocean drained and
sweat left on your pillowcase
face was under you and spat out milk

You make the coffee
dark
and pass it over
to me
the recognition in your look
like mud after rain
swirling 'round the cup

Hips

Cold tin against my
Soft skin
Pushing in the flesh
To straighten out my sides

You will decide

Bullet in your barrel
Who I am, who am I
Licking up my hips
With your wet wide mouth
You spit me out
You spit me out

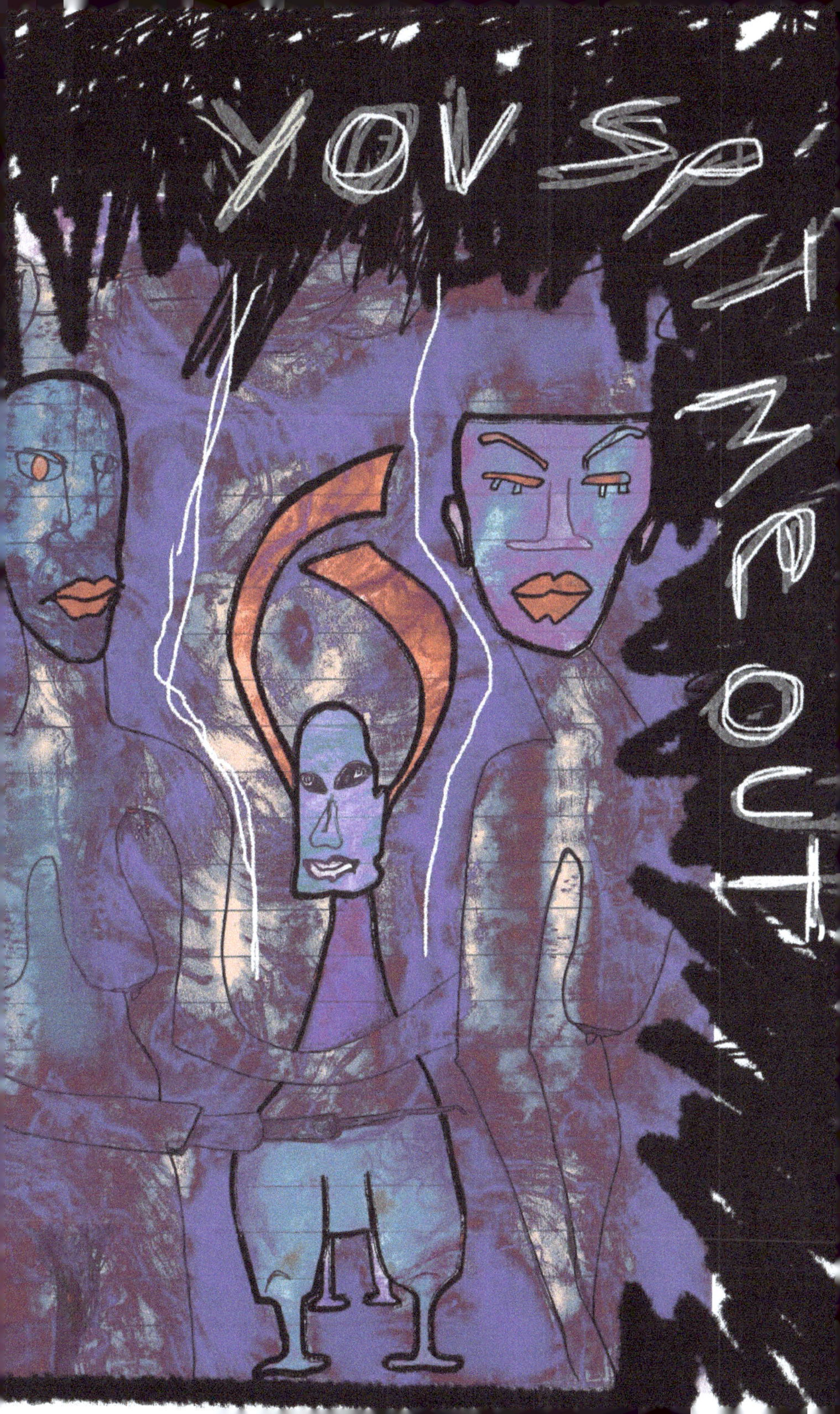
YOU SPIT ME OUT

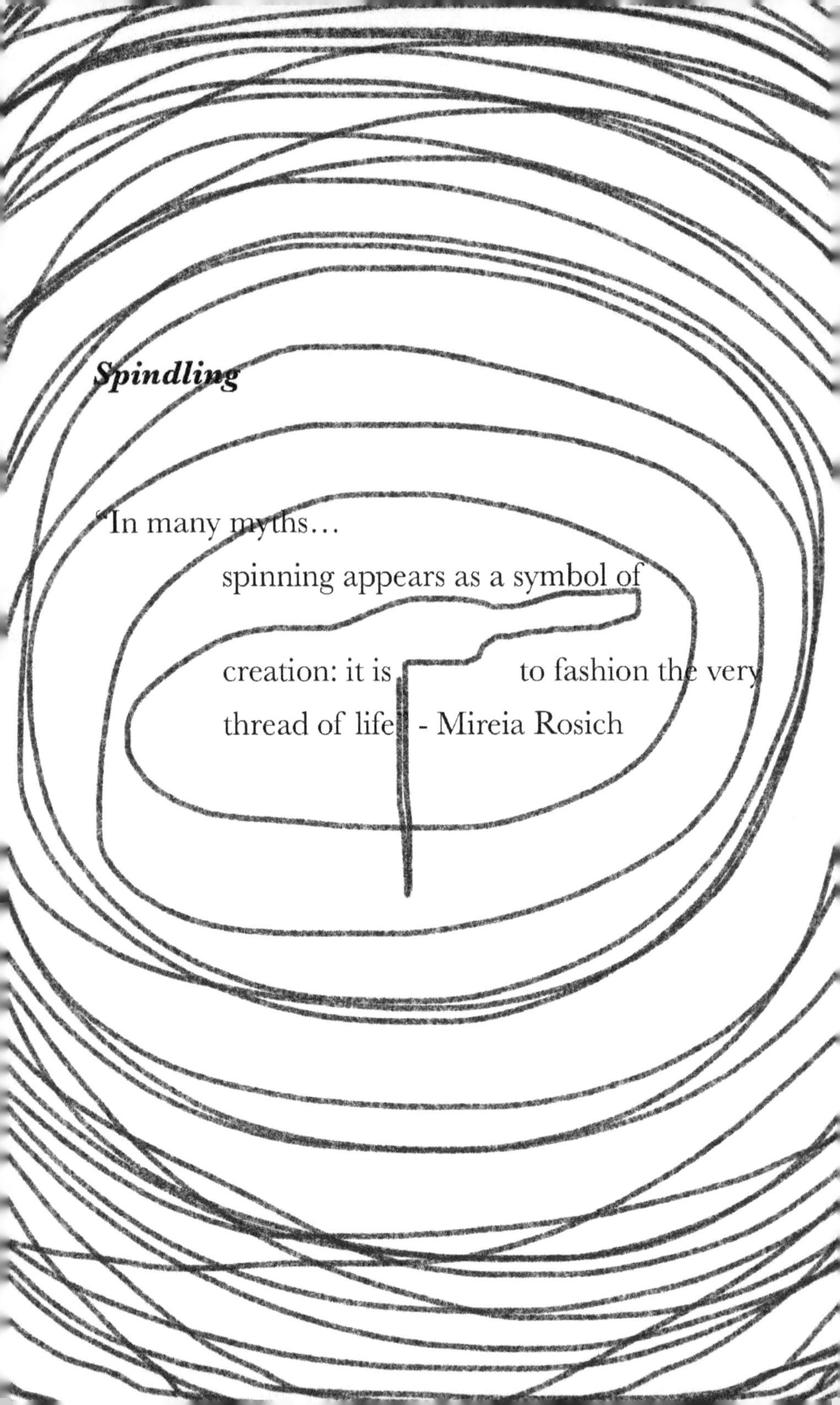

Spindling

"In many myths…

spinning appears as a symbol of

creation: it is   to fashion the very

thread of life" - Mireia Rosich

[Spin Unravel]

We hadn't known. Tonight we would confront that thing consuming us, walking past your house, spinning for some place to meet. 'Cause we hadn't *been* meeting, but hanging, around just around like cloud over the fell.

My chest began to flatten as our conversation fragmented, silence a sudden weight. It was some shameful secret slipping between our legs. We sat bent on the steps inside this new queer space. A Jazz duo wove through a crowd of conversations and I felt so alien. Our dissonance wasn't musical or interesting. Your reserved look shrunk me down and strung the night tighter. It grew loaded like a storm thick and grey.

Honesty draws us together as we speak of the unspoken. Your words are broken beneath milk blue. It rains a lot here, I heard.

Leg after leg
Stride outta focus
refuse to move over
edges / your words.
We hold hands and the air is narrow
Frustration grows hot inside
and shadows cup eyes
tired and taught feverish
The red wine / or some desire churns
below

too nauseous to look at you / to look at you and
not see you

Desire to leave / or desire to let go

The following morning felt silently aware, caught
in a circle, diameter between us
Heart aching for you

Out of bed, we seep into each other's mornings
(been a while)
Pancakes go running in the pan, we go running to
the bus
Sitting next to you makes it feel like a school trip.
our gazes grow softer, and
recognition floods my eyes
Tyres roll on beneath us

Wait on some steps whilst you search the market for
ripe fruit. Everything is dizzy eyes, moving across
the scene. The market bartering ricochets "one
pound a punnet!" and crowding feet. My look falls
to find your dusty brown boots. Perching on their
toes, creases like wrinkles telling time. They come
alive trailing behind the bar. Swivelling hips on a
dance floor, stepping a little closer. Treading over
cobbles into the morning. And the first time I kissed
you.

Return to me, bag full of fruit, strawberry punnet
in your hands. Skin feels like it'll melt when you're
around

/ / /
Time comes to meet your friend
Insecurity flies around like rubber bands, STING
You say i'm your baby and
It's ok
/ / /

Meeting the faces of others helps us unfold, I think.
Loosening our worlds, being two people and more.
Our circle unfolds into a land. Escaping the
uneasiness. Running for the bus, busting for a wee.
Pissing on the street. Our fates,
comfortably uncertain. That knot in myself
unwinds.

Taking off our clothes happens later, soon after you
pull out an antique map, catch my eyes, then pause,
your mouth widening to catch it.

"I can't believe I was about to pull out my map
when *you* are *on my bed*".

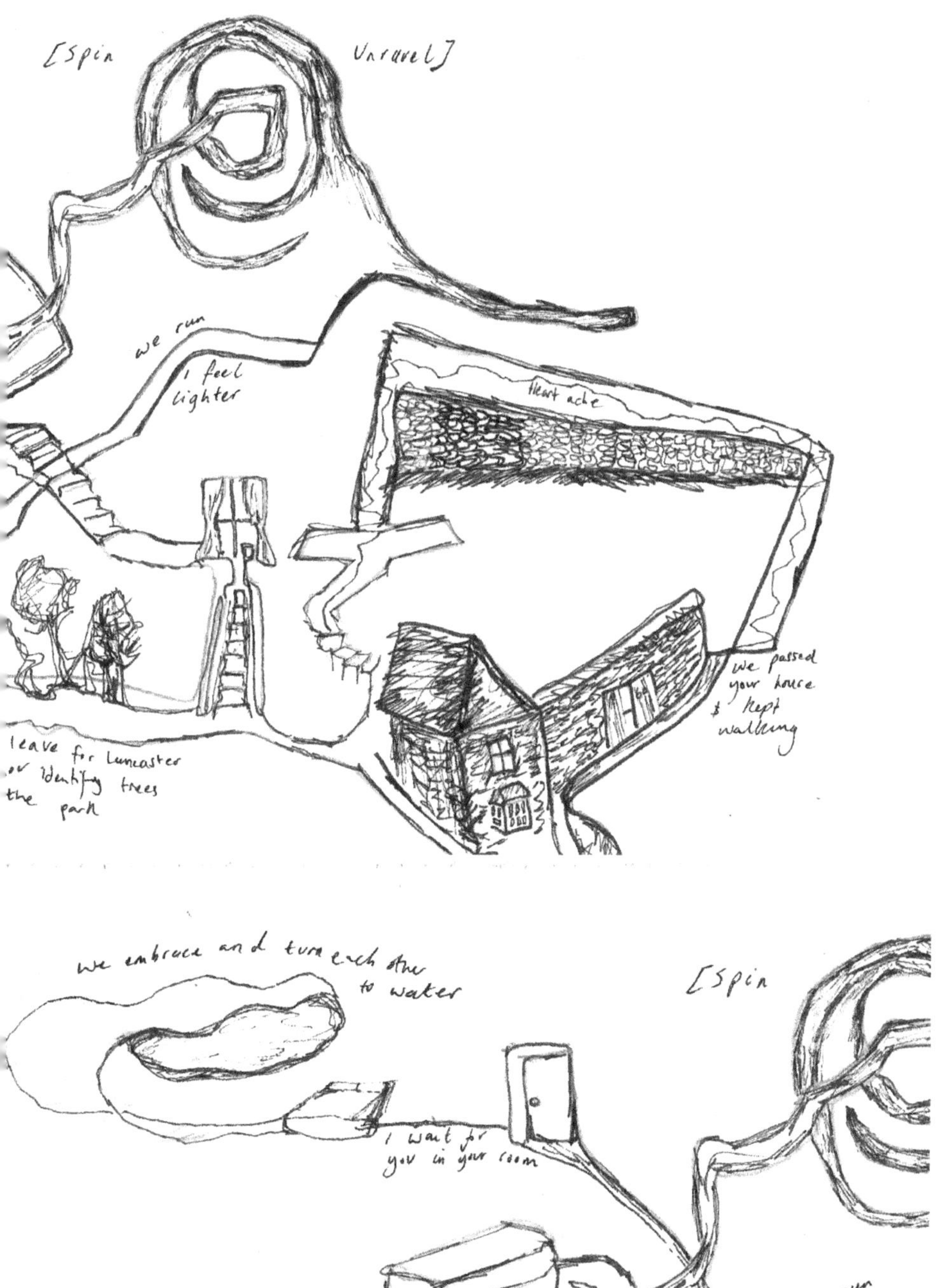

[Spin
Unravel]
we run
i feel lighter
Heart ache
leave for Lancaster
or Identify trees
the park
we passed your house.
& kept walking
we embrace and turn each other to water
[Spin
i wait for you in your room
we run
i feel lighter

clouds sit on the water's body
Our lips touch edges,
when the wind blows over
Mine under yours
the curling wet.
Hands fold 'round my belt buckle
white sky tucking in the black
Softened skin like a grass verge
everything borderless, borderless

Touch travels fast until
the zephyr's a gale:
You're over me
like a curving fist
torso pooling &
cloud falling in
The night meets us dead &
digging our walls out
as stillness calls to meet you
To meet you in the morning

Coffee Ritual

Bare ass
Nose stuffed
Stovetop alight
Octa-gon body in half
Soft ass sway on the fringes of my
tomb raider top
Am i Tomboy woman type (?)

Psychic Call

The shower is the right place to try something new. Months ago, we fell into each other's night at a bar. It had been elusive and momentary. Many other people had swept through my breath, stubbing out their butts to escape the cold and emptiness of early-night goodbyes. As I was stumbling over my words, talking to you, it was mid-december, mid gig. The outside was huddled under ten different conversations, pouring between liquid love or drunkenness. You, there, in front of me, and the openness to spill my guts. But the sound had gotten submerged and the air became glass right between us.

Bought a new body wash today, driven by an enlightenment that smelling like cedar wood would make all overthinking recede. Feeling suds wrap me up I swished the warm water round my mouth, and I spat you out into telephonic prayer.

"__lover_, _lover__, _lover__, hello".

I close my eyes right under the running water and picture you existing somewhere.

For a period of time during your degree and our first months together, we had talked about the U.S. in the 21st century. Its narratives had started revolving around brand power. "Disaster Capitalism," you had said. I later read about it. Republican policy makers were using crises to push neoliberal reforms under the guise of heroism.

"Since you broke my heart water bills have increased". "And the cedar wood market has exploded".

I grate the landscape of my shrivelled fingers. Your smile sits in my scrunched eyes. We can't be that far from each other.

"Can you hear me? Desire connects us. Desire and distress.".

Mid conversation I bend forward to relieve the tension. Curving spine and eyes down to the bathtub. From a bird's eye view it looks like the sink, and I feel my skin shred like cabbage down the drain. Nothing turns purple. Purple always was your colour.

Rain runs off my back like it's a table. I imagine you knocking a glass over me and the water spreading out. It would drip down through the wooden floor of our imaginary house, down into the holes of your inherited kitchen radio. It never makes it to our kitchen. In my mind I picture a fight scene. I'm turning like a ballerina through your voice, Leonard Cohen's melancholic joy sweeping 'round us.

"Are you Dancing to the End of Love?": ask the bathtub. Nose hangs close to my stomach, smelling the aroma of my new body wash.

Truth is I'm just spooling through the time, scrubbing away the clock, whilst you run your desire out into your own bathtub. There is no end.

I look down through legs, into the drain.
Underground my bathtub connects to yours.
You're crying out my shower head, &

water bills are rising.

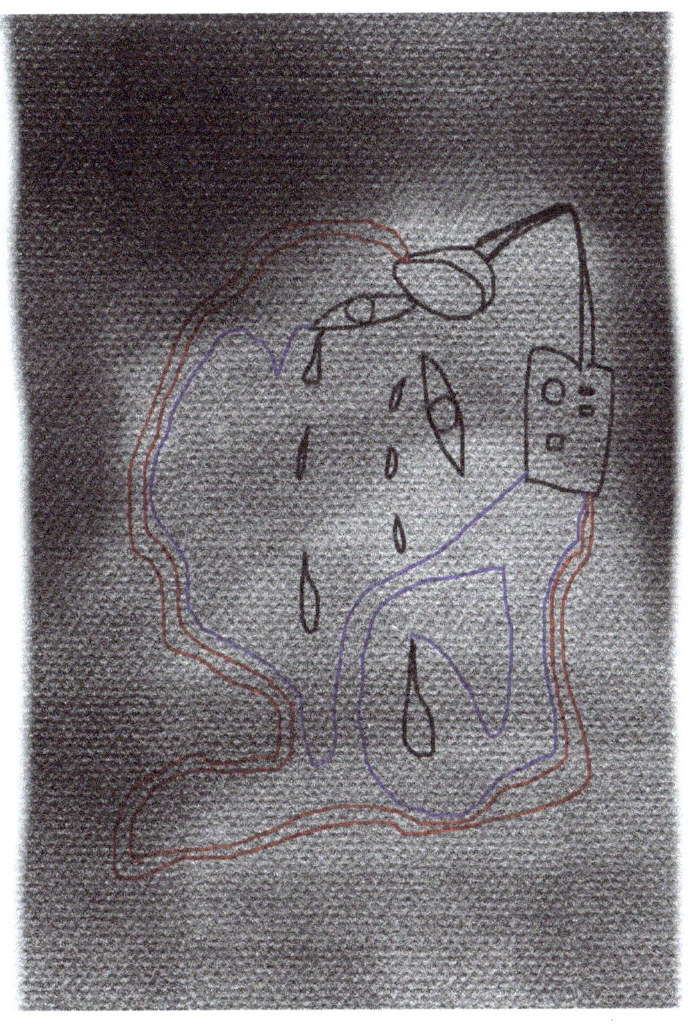

Supermarket

had a dream that two men were chasin'
at my heels for a lifetime
two bats
eyebrows low like fat
slugs
mouths open wide to eat the world
but
me first

saliva oozing out their smiles
the words fall out in sadistic gaps
"first slice, then mince, then roll up nice:
thumb pressed in the bottom of your back"
I never stopped runnin'
woke up
red oozing like sweat
like meat in the shop
lamb liver crying in
the folds of plastic
wrapped for display:
flesh for flesh
for sale

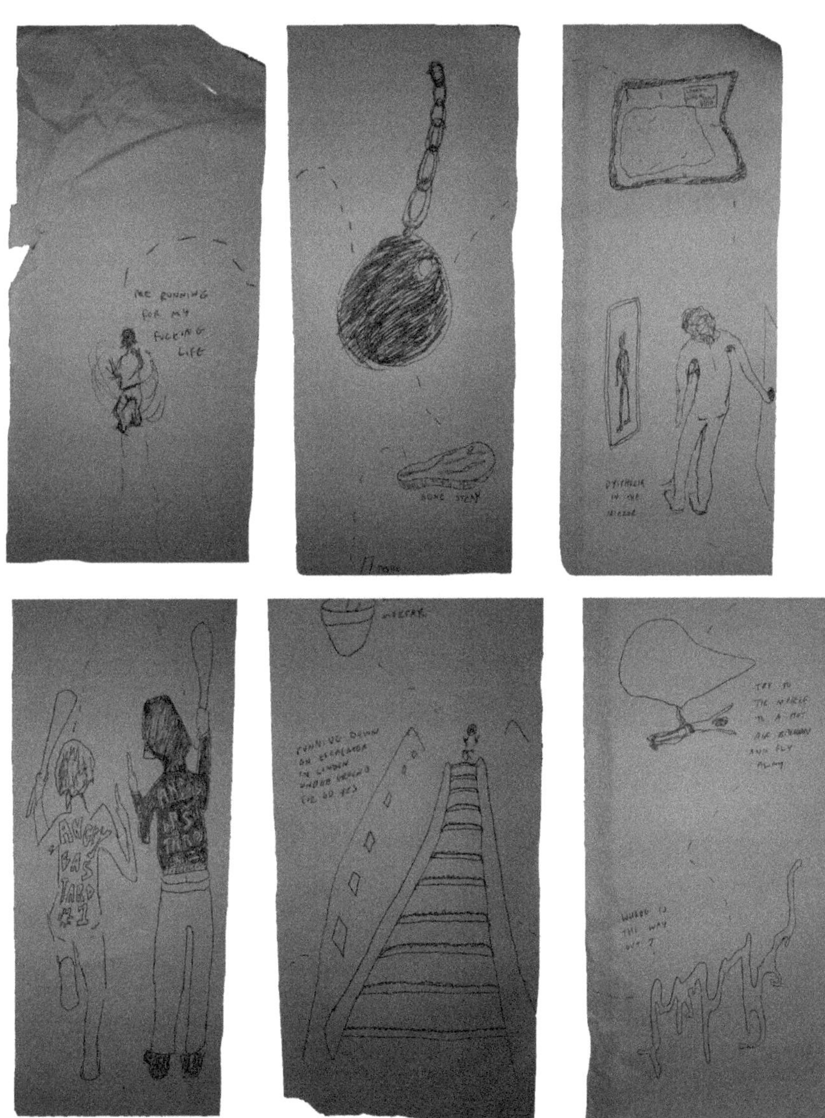

ME RUNNING FOR MY FUCKING LIFE
BONE STEAK
DYSTHYMIA IN THE MIRROR
ANGRY BASTARD #1
RUNNING DOWN AN ESCALATOR IN LONDON UNDERGROUND £12.60 YES
TIE IT TO THE KNIFE TIE A HOT AIR BALLOON AND FLY AWAY
WHICH IS THIS WAY OUT?

Truth is I'm Ugly

The last straight edge I saw was on my girlfriend's pocket knife, last night, when I was cutting my pubes in the hostel toilet. It was a one night getaway, passing through this sleepy city at the bottom of the world. Invercargill, New Zealand. Its half dilapidated body is pretty ugly to the eye. This industrial criss-cross, a has-been. Impossible to be consumed in. Boredom expected for visitors passing through, except if you're there for a dyke affair, ofc.

~~Apologies to anyone who is permanently content in Invercargill.~~ Apologies to anyone not eating out women up the stairs of an old hospital. It was the cheapest private room around, galvanised by the smell of cigarettes up the stairwell, glossed with speckled vinyl and the transience of our stay. Quick to greet my lover, I ran heavy on the steps, pushing myself further into the womb of ~~tackiness~~ greatness.

The truth is, i'm ugly, and that's what gives me the audacity, you know.

It's something in the ugly
folding 'round my death
making something out -
protecting
half-formed understandings
of what i am

is the city;
raining into the fissures
of my leather
like it just knows
that ugliness prevails
and that i don't suffer
when queer sex with my
lover
unfurls all the insides
residing in our breaths
to be seen,
alive
Rivers coursing in the city

Third Place/Piss Jeans

They told me about Shibari at the bar. We were
meeting again after a year apart. And the last time
we'd met was the first. I learned: It was usual to tie
up your friends. Their face was freckled and copper
under the light. Outside was sticky enough for leath-
er and a shirt. They'd come from the station with
a suitcase full of CBD and a guitar barely opened.
Next to me they split the night. Defining conver-
sation. Maybe I was just in love with the way they
rocked back the chair as they spoke hands above
their head retelling being tied. How it's common
to hang and tie your friends. It wasn't gruesome or
violent. It was a way to open 'self space' they said.
It wasn't sex, or fucking the night through. It was
tenderness and it was hot. It was folding and sus-
pending and asking with each touch. Is this what
you want? Like twisting a body into a path. Or
stretching back against the air. Like this Third Place
you go. In the van of a guy 49 or 50. And weirdness
wasn't in the fabric of it. Believe me. I was begin-
ning to trust the plane of their words so I spread out
and said how I always wanted to know that feeling
of suspension. And the rub and the contorting.
Of the me I hated and wanted tortured. 'Cause it
felt so good. To sink and be held. That third place
under my porous skin. That third place seeping in
and running down the road. It's stuffing up with the

need to be seen. This third place I want it fucking
everywhere. Free and intimate.

....

Put your piss
in my jeans

Does that work?

Put your belly
in my sick

Put your feet
in my dance

Put your denim
in my mouth

Tough

Put your hands
in my phone

Put your tongue
out my -

No

Put your stomach
in my drink

Sip sip

Put your Hi in my Bye

Smoke that
cigarette and
ash on
the glass

Put your fag
in my spit

Light it

Put your boyfriend
in the dump

Put your turn
in my jump

Catch my look
from above

Come down
from the gig

Put your man
in my boot

Stomp stomp

Put your purple

in the door
frame

Put your veins
on my road
          meet me

Put the train
in my leg
          step down

Put your brain
in my jeans
          yes, that

Put the bitch
in my bike
          alright?

Put your fist
through my T.V
          we're out

Put your jeans
in my piss

Just

Put your bladder
in my house

Barry McGee

Loneliness is the common denominator. Lingering in empty landscapes. Teething on post-break up adrenaline hikes. Most are sad but haven't admitted it. Pull down the shutters to defend myself from the heat. Cicadas sing and the room is swallowed in mid-day darkness. I'm pushed to recall everything. It's like one of those brain teaser game shows from the 80s, except I am remembering lost queer loves instead of bananas. The host of the show is the only long-standing resident of the room, a daddy-long legs who I've named Barry. Barry happens to have extreme capacity for empathy and expansive knowledge on contemporary queer theory. He's the billie piper to my david tennant in time travelling spirals of memory and longing. Long-legs for longing, and back outstretched, ready for siesta.

I haven't napped so spontaneously since the womb
TALK about holiday and capital doom
breaks only happen in my back
travel agencies get off on work-life crack

Inner peace is monetized
when i pour pints in performative time
Money by Flink Poyd Plays
& boot slaps the gas of the dime

cowboy heels tappin'
the bar stool
was broken in by the ass of
a 9-5   clerk named phil
whose only claim to fame
is sellin pills
& how quick he scans the SPAM
for the gammon man

We're all in a game of role plays and deals
naming our kids after supermarket chains
FUCKIN' FEEEEEL

                         something!

mind forged manacles said william blake
what a flake for lingering
on that
line

Where's the key will? what's the plan?
Phil offers up his pocket ham
whilst I reach in
pockets dusty filled with crap
some FAT£9/hour stack
                (i've been here since 1982)

Dishin out thanks to those
I serve
Tits for Tips

don't wanna kiss you, sir

The immortal loop of being bar-stuck
& star-struck at
My Commitment to The Role

if only I could waltz to Janis Joplin
alone in my
home

Me and my Barry McGee

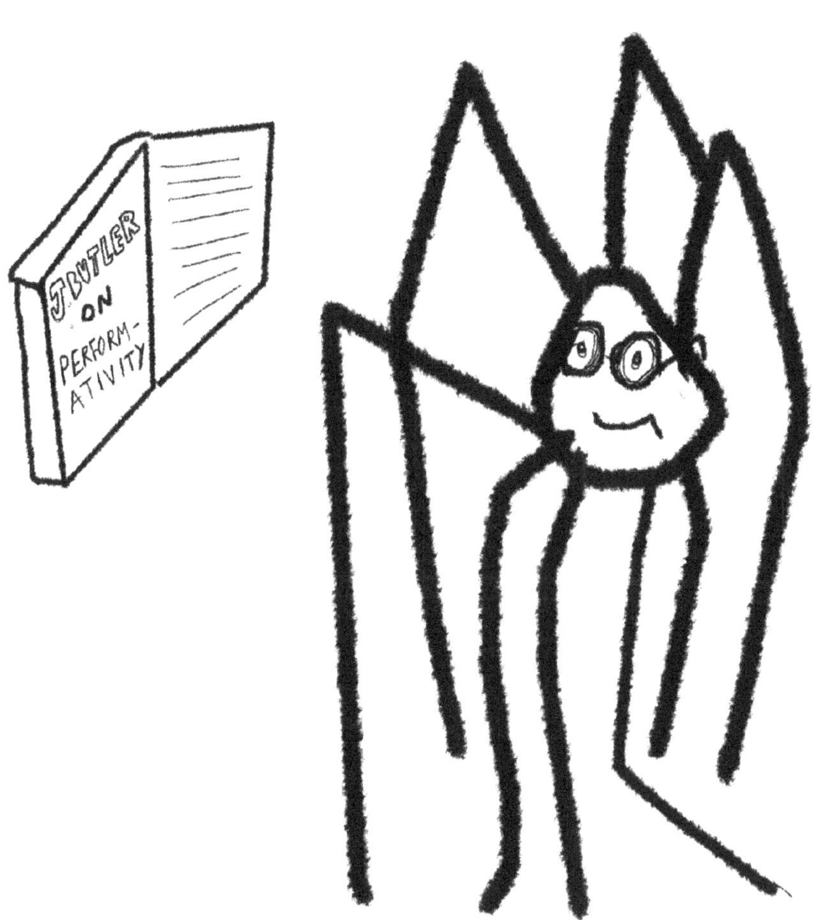

Landlord Ashes

A slap-the-artery habit for caffeine - and for my lover, her crochet - is unstoppable, inevitable, stained & inseparable as I handle the mug and she picks up the needle. In the city I move with inertia

Swish
    Swishhh
                Slap

Slap

Sometimes, the habit catches me in a better way. In the insides of a falling apart home and the cavern of my friend's morning sounds. We screech at each other as a signal for good-morning-put-the-coffee-on. Wweeeeeeeaaaghhhhh. We are whales peeking heads above water to greet each other. Bleary eyed and barely born, slimy backs sharp in the light peeping 'round the curtain pleats.

I wait outside for the signal

Today
smells different
like plasterboard &
pieces

discovered my whale
like a foetus   under it

barely born
& silent

Supermarket, 3.1.24

You look good. Yes, I like you. Finger in the net, I pull them up from their crate.
Well you look like a mess.
Rind scrapes my finger edges; course words, course skin. I wonder when you're gonna call.
I tell the oranges that I got the upper hand, lips pursed: a quick witted aside. Look at them
hanging all shy and defeated. HA. I uncurl my finger and they tumble from two feet into the
basket. I love food shopping 'cause I'm in charge. Well, mostly. Sometimes cruel noises like
YUCK crawl into the aisles and lay across me like a spider. Chin to my chest, eyes to my
belly. But it's way worse waiting for your call. When I make the first move light bleeds
through me and you got the lines to close me up.
Leaving the supermarket with a basket full is POWER. Where's my parent? Don't need 'em.
Load up my power into my bike box and that bag that hangs awkwardly on the side. An extra
limb. Maybe I'll grow an extra limb with all this nourishment. Hand curves around a chickpea
can like a first embrace. My extra limb gets heavier and heavier. Everything topples
sideways with a crash bang, cans clinking and it's all kinda thrilling. Like when you've just
fucked someone new and they leave. (Hey look!) there's all my power on the wet pavement.
Chickpea tin rolling over the glimmering black. Street light casts a tide over the scene and all
my misery is like a TV on fire. You still haven't called. Housemate comes back outside and
sees the gawky stranger who sped to my rescue. Your erm basket erm isn't balanced. I don't
have another erm bungee on me. His erms are charming and unnerving all at once. I
imagine a green creature under his skin called ERM. Louis offers to house my power in his
shopping bags. There's room. I offer the bread over to be next to his bread saying thanks
darling, it's a bread bag now. That's what everyone at work calls each other. What bread
bag? No, darling. It's the weird intimacy of chefs I gather. Pet names and hard hands. Louis'
hands are all cracked up like a desert path. Lots of old cuts, dried blood. All the wrinkles
have become hinges. I wanna touch them and make them soft. The pavement twinkles
beneath us as we walk home. The dark seals around me. Blood dried and light sewn in.

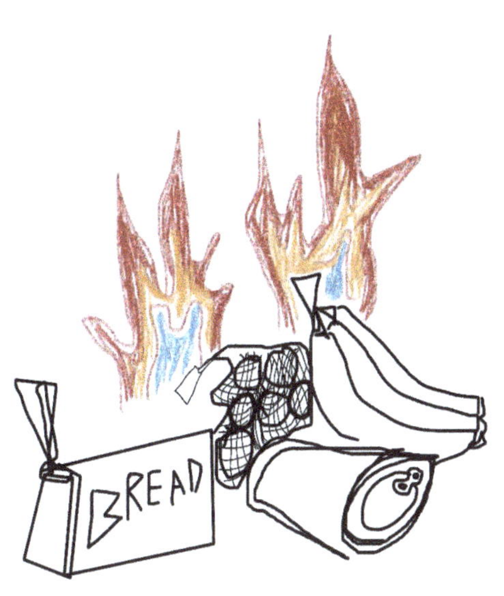
BREAD

Eat

It is hard to know what unfurls
in your mind
when you see
these lines
that run along my
breast bone

I call it that
not 'cause breasts are there
but
'cause it bears
arches of
worry

When you look
you see
pools
of black

ambiguous enough
to step in
but
on terms that
were grown
long before your
birth

It is hard to know how
heavy
the de-
marca-
tion
lands
Do you
take my
landscape
with hands
fusty
from
father's
tongue

Your most
rotten
comes
in
sickly
sweet
terms

It's hard
to
know

if you write
feminine
into the way
you fuck me

So dainty
though
if i were
to pin you
below

Thighs squeeze
to nothing
It's hard to know
if you
would use
and choose
this
toughness
as
glass to
pass
through

Tantalising
huh

this
chance to
work your
Daddy
issues

No

I'm not
these lines
for you

But

It's hard
to know
if that
hunger
in your
look
is true
Do you want me
Or do you want
you

If you are this city then where am I

when I stop
looking for you
in these alleyways
breath is held
and i
birth sighs
into the business

cheeks hot
chin leaning on
all stories you
led me
into

here by this
church you put
your face on my
face

this city begs to be full
without you

Inside

Opening up that space
Daytime wide n different
After she looked inside
Touched something
Touched everything

God - cry into the afternoon

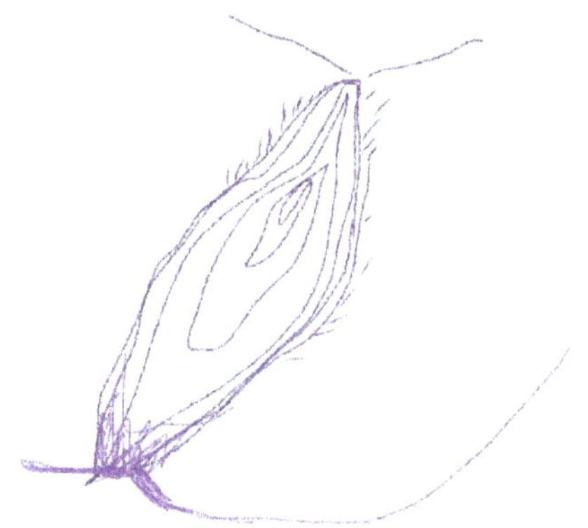

Capacity

spongey lost my
water
been tryna clean
your
acheyness

energy
like tryna gather
from a sticky
kitchen floor
loving is only possible
When you leave
Me
First

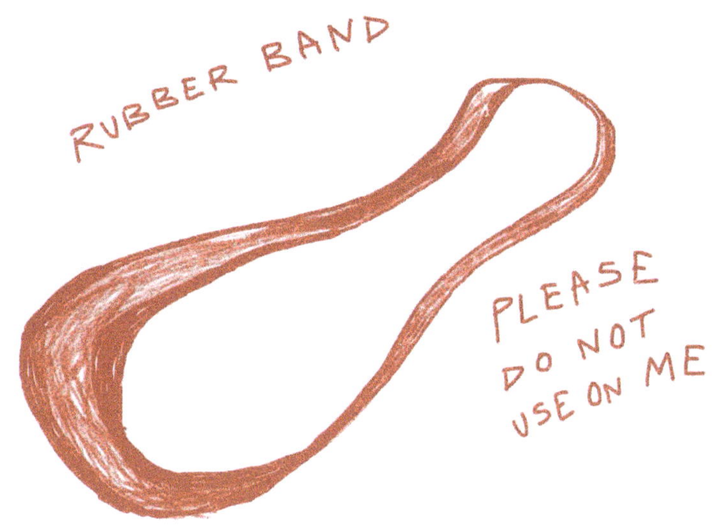

RUBBER BAND
PLEASE
DO NOT
USE ON ME

There's a chance i could be pregnant

Our intimacy has not left me with a child
unless
anxiety grows arms
two legs
a body -
Yours' was a furnace so
broad your
breadth
split open and
slacked;
you didn't make me
fem - i - nin.
'what do you want'
i test
'turn on your front';
You just
murmured
moaned
when i kissed you
like some baby bird
begging
The night was a string
a power line - we
moved along
sipping the
question of

is this
you
i want
It is
so much that
skin's oozing off n
i forget
stranger you're
a man
in my bed
N' i'm burnin up in
the hours left
the dark this puddle
bathing in sweat
'cause
intimacy scares the
shit […]
I bleed out
something
legs red as you
leave
Morning's dry as i
suck on
the memory
eat eat
'till fantasy
GAGS

pregnant with this life
wet, viscid knees
A child may be these
lovers i don't leave
behind

Every Saturday

curtain pole,
radio,
kitchen glass n'
garden.
patio,
rhythm go,
mum dancing
on the carpet
daddio
daddio
your teeth
got gaps
green n' brown
don't make a
sound as you
pull up on
the driveway
that gravel growl
an ocean howl
you're this iceberg
'round my sea
your ship
pale red Audi
a ghost at
the window

curtain pole
radio/
engine breaks the
morning
you sit
wait for me
and this
whole life my
short legs
go
wiry, cold

My Love For You Is

  as real as
  a femur snapping in two

And the oozing in its gap
Like mouths full of toothpaste and no sink
Bulging cheeks and watery eyes
As real as
forks scraped across porcelain
Like lungs in water and black in the sun

Idols & IBS

Idols
I make them
& shit
out
myself
squatting over
the white ring
consumed
by
shame
as guts
shake
all that
slimy trouble
you've got none
of it
your perfect
shit
stomach a
lake
flat
my friend says
that
trauma
is
the torrent
blowing
about
our gut

how IBS
is a form
it takes
"like crying
or
dancing
or
idolizing
in your
case"

I*dolize*
B*oyfriends*
S*yndrome*

though
it's not
boys
or
girls
it's women
and all those
mother issues
growling
bowel
growling
arching
over the
naked

crouch
so vulnerable
here as i
shit you out
self
hatefulness
twisting
my lover
you
are never
twisting
perfectly still
& rooted
that ground
your toes
are made
from
Your children
will be sunflowers
and not
fucked up at
All

What are
mummy issues
let's unpack
friend unjoins
her hands
as if to
make room

It's needing
her to
need me
but need
my need
is untrue
not expressed
as
a
word
carrying
meaning
just an
aching twirp
a dying
bird
a
NEEEEEEEEEED
He-ar
me
under the
branches
arches
of
all that
history
history is blood
in your
belly
mum

& lack of
it
that month
you
realised
I was
inside
taking up
some
     Your life
guilt is a gut
in the toilet bowl

did you howl
& scream
& shake
when i was
born
did it
somehow
rip your
wallpaper
into rough
rhine
fingertips along it
the danger
the dangerousness
& a soft
fleshy
thing
your arm holding

I was this
chubby
being
born into
the world
marshmallow
pleated puppiness
HUGE hazel eyes
did you
see my
eyes
mum
mellow you said
i was
but i had skin
enough to
hide

hiding now
in
the pleats of my lover's beauty
& the itch
gets quick
they wanna
spit me out
saliva is thick [though]
they have truly
loved me

To escape that
hum
throbbing beneath their chin
i would rest
head on breast
squawking
bleeding out
that
NEEEEEEEEEEED
seeping into
them
eyes fast
on
bedroom
wall
small &
smaller
shrink to
aeroplane pose
on toilet bowl
forehead to knees
did you ever
see me
mum
did you ever see
in those big
hazel
eyes

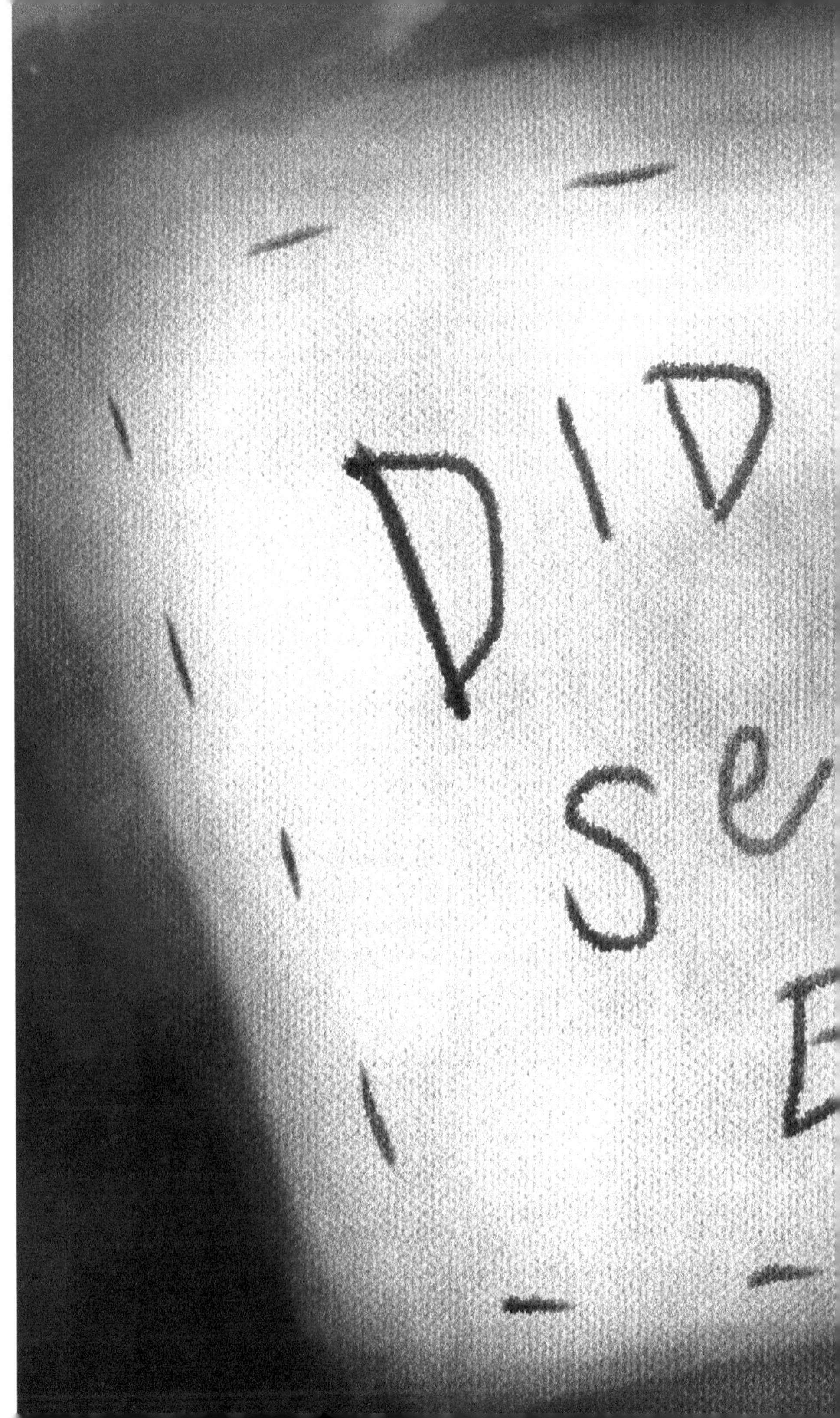
DID
Se
S
E

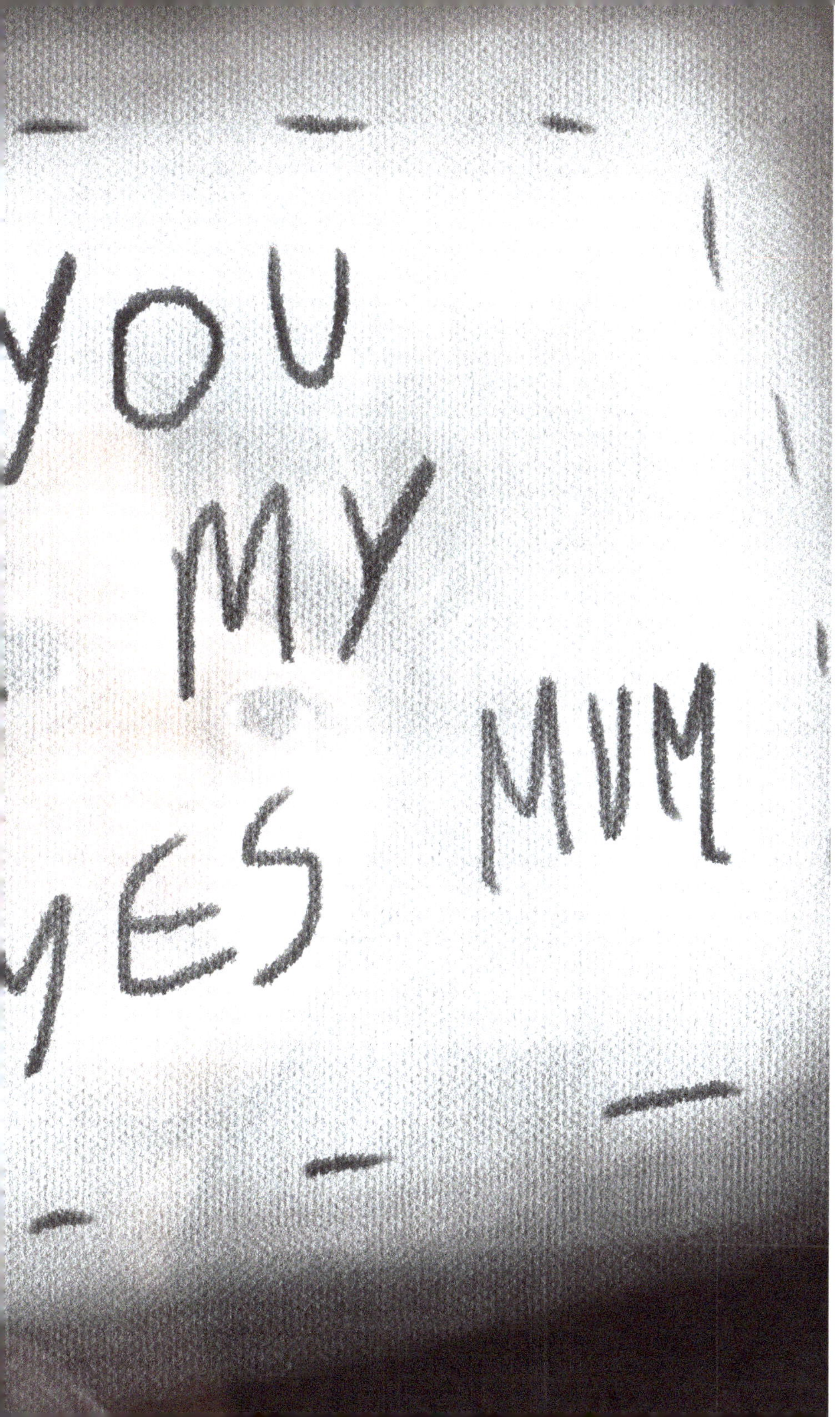
YOU
MY
YES MUM

About Jazzy

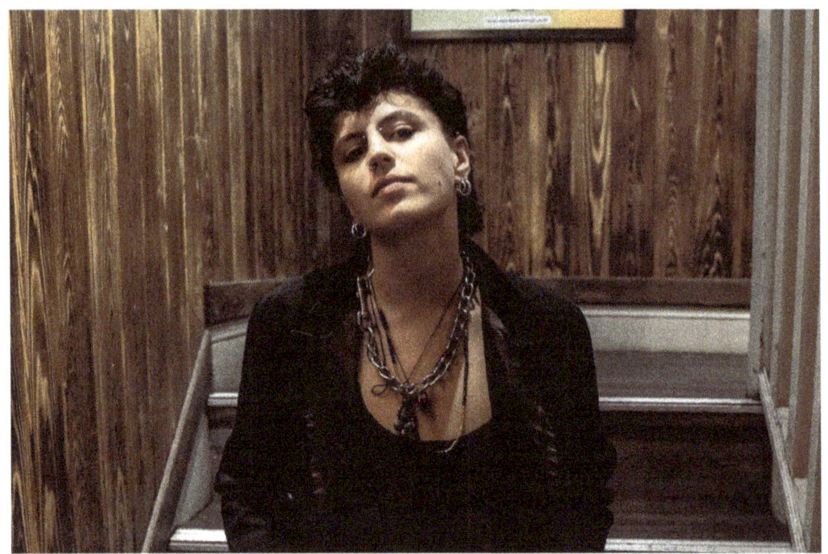

photo by **Frances Fox**

Jazzy Green hangs their hat, as well as their heart, just about anywhere they land. Poetry, for them, has always been a means to understand being, in all its forms, beyond the academic institution. Trying to shape a voice that's real in a sea of contra-sounds is a journey forever unfolding, and one that must be, they believe, stamped by all that they are. Their words aim to be relentless, unapologetic marks, like cigarettes stubbed onto your skin. Then sometimes, afterwards, a kiss of forgiveness; a breath or a break. Themes that pervade are entirely entangled and this is how they wish to be seen. Anxious attachment, neoliberalism, consumption, queer desire, absence and fullness; within the knot, they hope there's something you can find. For more of their work, see 'Slimy Mind', a substack publication that has absolutely no schedule and thus comes raw. They also endorse your fully fledged support for New Words Press, who are re-writing the boundaries of publishing in its links to capitalism and heteronormativity and so much more. Come along for the ride and everything you don't know yet.

About nw{p}

new words {press} is a non-profit poetry press publishing trans* & gender-expansive poets & hybrid writers.

support our efforts & the incredible writers we publish. visit us at

newwordspress.com

new words {press}
A TRANS* & GENDER-EXPANSIVE POETRY PRESS